The Master's Call

Steve Williams

The Master's Call by Steve Williams © 2015 by John Marshall

This book or parts thereof may not be reproduced in any form, stored in a retrieval system or transmitted in any form by any means—electronic, mechanical, photocopy, recording or otherwise—without prior written permission of the publisher, except as provided by United States of America copyright law.

Scripture quotations marked KJV are taken from the Holy Bible, King James Version (Public Domain).

Scripture quotations marked NKJV are taken from the New King James Version®. Copyright ©1982 by Thomas Nelson. Used by permission. All rights reserved.

Scripture quotations marked NLT are taken from the Holy Bible, New Living Translation copyright ©1996, 2004, 2007 by Tyndale House Foundation. Used by permission of Tyndale House Publishers Inc., Carol Stream, IL 60188. All rights reserved. New Living, NLT, and the New Living Translation logo are registered trademarks of Tyndale House Publishers.

Scripture quotations marked NASB are taken from the New American Standard Bible®, Copyright ©1960, 1962, 1963, 1968, 1971, 1972, 1973, 1975, 1977, 1995 by The Lockman Foundation Used by permission. (www.Lockman.org)

Scripture quotations marked NIV are taken from the THE HOLY BIBLE, NEW INTERNATIONAL VERSION®, NIV® Copyright ©1973, 1978, 1984, 2011 by Biblica, Inc.TM Used by permission. All rights reserved worldwide.

Scripture quotations marked NRSV are taken from the New Revised Standard Version Bible, copyright ©1989 the Division of Christian Education of the National Council of the Churches of Christ in the United States of America. Used by permission. All rights reserved.

Scripture quotations marked NAB are taken from the New American Bible, revised edition ©2010, 1991, 1986, 1970 Confraternity of Christian Doctrine, Washington, D.C. and are used by permission of the copyright owner. All Rights Reserved. No part of the New American Bible may be reproduced in any form without permission in writing from the copyright owner.

Scripture quotations marked ESV are from the ESV Bible® (The Holy Bible, English Standard Version®), copyright ©2001 by Crossway Bibles, a publishing ministry of Good News Publishers. Used by permission. All rights reserved. http://www.crossway.org.

© 2015 by John Marshall

All rights reserved

ISBN: 978-0-9820475-6-9   0-9820475-6-8

Printed in the United States of America

TABLE OF CONTENTS

Dedications and Acknowledgements vii
Preface xi

Chapter 1:   Introduction 13
Chapter 2:   Viewing Religion with a Skeptical Eye . . 19
Chapter 3:   Losing Interest 21
Chapter 4:   The Master's Call. 29
Chapter 5:   Life Isn't Making Sense. 35
Chapter 6:   Headed into the Unknown 39
Chapter 7:   The Cancer Returned 45
Chapter 8:   Nothing Comes Easy 51
Chapter 9:   Am I Convinced?. 55
Chapter 10: A Therapist or Preacher? 59
Chapter 11: Know Your Limitations 65
Chapter 12: An Interest or Destiny? 69
Chapter 13: She Fell Asleep, and I Learned a
             Valuable Lesson on page 79

Some Final Words 85
References 87

DEDICATIONS AND ACKNOWLEDGEMENTS

I dedicate this book to God my father, Jesus my Saviour, The Holy Spirit my power and guide, Evelyn Kaye Williams, my loving wonderful wife and Braylon, the greatest grandson and friend an old man could ever have.

Kaye, you took on a great challenge in marrying me. When you first decided to date me, my life was partially broken and unsure. You didn't give up on me (although at times, I felt like giving up), and you have made me a better man, minister, father, husband and grandfather. Your loving patience along with God's instructions have made me into the husband I am. Your smile has brought sunshine into an otherwise cloudy day; going to sleep by your side and waking up to your smile have brought me nothing but joy, laughter and peace. I live a better life because of Jesus but I sleep better because of you. Outside of God, I will never love another as much as I love you.

Braylon, papa's baby and closest friend. The first day I laid eyes on you. "It was on." You chose me that day. Others wanted to hold you, but you came and felt comfortable only with me. The first words you said, when you came to my house, "where is my papa?" When I was sweating, after I preached, you took my handkerchief and dried my face. When you ate your meal, you made sure papa had something to eat from your plate. When we first arrived in the church's auditorium, the first thing you did was head for the microphone. You would ask me to help you get the microphone; there you would sing and preach your heart out. If you grow up to be a singer or preacher, I will not be surprised. It appears they were in your genes from your youth. And more than that, they appeared to be gifts from heaven. Please use them well. You may discover you have an Achilles heel, but God will empower you to overcome. Your future looks bright; you ought to Praise God with your life.

To my children, you have been more than great, you have been wonderful. Nikia, Ian, and Tarquinn, don't forget who started you in this race. It was Jesus, "the author and finisher of our faith" (Hebrews 12:2 KJV). I have been blessed to be your father and I cherished every moment. God has a plan for each of you. Don't be afraid to live your lives for Jesus because he lived and died and organized a plan for you (Ephesians 2:10 KJV). As much as I know and breathe God's air, God has placed you on the right path in the gospel and body of Christ. Don't leave his path to investigate the paths of others because God knows which path you belong. Make God and your grandpa proud. You are the best as long as you remain in Christ (Ephesians 1:3; 2:6 KJV).

PREFACE

———•———

The phone rang and rang; for a week it rang; and for a week John failed to answer. John later learned he won a lucrative prize but forfeit it because he fail to answer. Millions of prizes are lost annually in this country because people fail to claim them. That phone call you ignored; that knock on the door you fail to answer; that person you bumped into who wanted to talk, but you didn't have time could have been more than incidents. They could have been "The Master's Call."

The Master is calling

"Sometimes it's not incidents but providence."

SW

"For many are called, but few are chosen."

Matt 22:14 (KJV)

Chapter 1

INTRODUCTION

I am now 66 years of age; an old man and wondering where all the time went. My earliest reflection was one of as a two or three year old baby boy. I remember following my grandfather as he plowed the field preparing it for seeding. Those early days in North Carolina were the formative years that help shape me into the man I am today. My mother was a gentle good looking woman, and my father was strict, hard working and said to be a lady's man. They started their marriage and family at a young age in Portsmouth Virginia. They tried to make their marriage work but failed. I guess sometime love isn't enough. When mom and dad separated, mom became the custodial parent, but my brother and I floated between both of them until our early teens. During this time, we became too rambunctious for mom; so she sent us to live with our father in Portsmouth (my mom lived in Washington DC until her death, and my father remained in Virginia until his death).

Every summer my older brother and I found ourselves in the tobacco fields of North Carolina visiting and working with our grandfather. But I did more visiting than working because I was the knee baby and too little to work; so I was told. Just before my mom and dad separated, these series of images remained chiseled in my mind—especially one disturbing encounter of my father. My father and my uncle were on foot chasing a man. I was running trying to keep up. I guess I was approximately five or seven. Why was I chasing my father and uncle? I guess I felt a bond with them, especially my father. The chase led into a partially lit alley way. There my daddy and uncle cornered that man. My father pulled a gun and placed it in that man's chest. He pulled the trigger once or twice, but the gun misfired. My father gave the man a few choice words and he and my uncle turned and walked away. I don't know what the argument was about but I was glad my father didn't kill that man. If he had, my life probably would have been altered

Introduction

forever. I was relieved because my daddy wasn't going to jail. What happened to that man? Well I never saw him again. I hope he learned something from that encounter. God gave him and my father a second chance. Until this day, I still have images of that eventful day. But two things seem to always stand out in those imageries, the narrowness of the alley way and the light at the end of the alley. My life has become one dedicated to walking in the narrow way to reach heaven. I guess miracles still do happen.

After separating, my mom and dad didn't speak very much to one another unless it was in regards to my brother and me. But my father held a profound respect for my mother. Mom never knew it but you could see in his eyes how warm he felt about her when he spoke of her from time to time. Dad never divorced my mom even after more than twenty years of separation. Dad's relationship with my mom taught me, if you find a good woman, don't allow her to slip from your life because you may live to regret it. I am sure my Dad did. And my mom never got over my father; whenever she spoke of him, her face lit up and went from a flicker to a flame. The lesson that still lingers, embossed in my mind was how much my father and mom loved one another but something in their past crippled their future together. Another lesson I took from their relationship was sometimes you only get one chance at love; so learn to forgive because the best could be yet to come.

The most vivid picture I have of my grandfather was of a man who could do no wrong. He attended church on Sundays and when he didn't, I observed him, under the oak tree in the front yard, listening to church service on the radio. One day that portrait of a perfect grandfather was shattered and altered. Someone cried out "Fed man." The house was stirring and people were running. I looked for my grandfather but he was nowhere in the house. I looked out the window and there was grandfather with two huge empty jugs in hand, picking them up and putting them down. I did know an old man could run so fast. It appears grandfather was in the moonshine business on the side to subsidize his farming income. After that day, when I looked at my grandfather, it was with eyes of doubt and confusion. I never stopped loving him, but I was unsure of who he was. I guess the old adage is true, "you can't judge a book by its cover." You don't know some people as well as you think. You have no real clue who they are. Perhaps, they are normal people who break the law occasionally. But whoever my grandfather was, his life made an impact upon mines; until this day, I can't shake the old guy.

Chapter 2

VIEWING RELIGION WITH A SKEPTICAL EYE

I viewed religion with an eye of skepticism. As a young teenager, I didn't attend worship very much. But the times I visited with my family, I found the preaching hard to understand. The preacher had a cadence sound; the church enjoyed it, but it added to my difficulty understanding his message.

Most days after school, I spent with my friend Bubble. Bubble was tall and lean and suffered from asthma. He smoked, drank beer and gambled on occasions. But though Bubble and I were close, I wasn't influenced very much by his life. One day out of the blue, and not as I planned,

I told Bubble "I am going to church next Sunday." That Sunday came, and I did attend worship but Bubble didn't (I always wondered why I chose to attend that Sunday and Bubble didn't). Now that I look back on that choice, it slowly created a distant between Bubble and me. Neither I nor Bubble wanted the change or our relationship to end. But change came through our lives like a summer storm, and there was nothing we could do about it. It appears that some relationships are destined to end. You see, Bubble died around the age of 33 of a drug overdose. If we had remained friends, my life could have ended in the same way.

Chapter 3

LOSING INTEREST

I soon lost interest in school and, it appeared, my father's live-in girl friend and I were not on the best of terms. She was pushing and my thoughts were, "You are not my mother; stop pushing" (But the truth be told I was doing more resisting than she was pulling and she did me more good than hurt). My father recognized the tension between us. He told me if I couldn't live by his rules, I could leave, and so I did. But I never held a grudge against my father. I never challenged him on issues I thought he was wrong, such as his splitting with my mother or placing his girl friend before his children. I knew such challenges would be suicide! (I got to give it to the old man. He didn't permit his children, though he loved us, to spoil his personal happiness. And in the long run, my father's mind-set ended up becoming a blessing to me. So children, don't be so hard on your parents. Their choices could be your blessings.)

I quit high school, took the military exam, passed, and entered the Marine Corps. My father was happy for me, and I was finally happy to leave home. What else can you do with a teenage boy feeling his testosterone and on a collision with his father? I guess God knew something I didn't (a course, he did). But whatever it was, he knew I could no longer live under the same roof with my father and his girl friend. I guess I viewed her as trying to take the place of my mother, and that wasn't going to happen. It appeared she had a strong sense of needing to be in control (like most parents or acting parents) and I had a strong impulse not to allow anyone to control me who wasn't my parent. Later, I would grow up to feel very differently about her. The truth be known, she helped save my life from the streets while I was growing up. And, after you got to know her, she was very pleasant.

One fall day, I left I.C. Norcom High School in Portsmouth Virginia. One of the things I hated about that departure was leaving a sweet little girl by the name of Zipporah with whom I had grown mesmerized. She would later have a major impact in my life. I entered military basic training. I was informed I would be going to Viet Nam shortly thereafter. I knew what that meant. I probably wouldn't be returning home alive. So I cut all contact with all my girls including Zipporah. I thought "why should my death become a sad detraction in their lives?"

In 1968 I was officially in the Republic of South Viet Nam trying to save the South from a Northern communist invasion but that wasn't to be. Sometimes, the only person you can save is yourself and sometimes, you can't do that without the help of others. I think we were miss guided in trying to help South Viet Nam. We ended up losing the war and getting kicked out of the country. Hopeful, we learned we can't force our moral and political views upon others. After I had been in country about six months, I received a surprise letter from Zipporah. I wondered what she wanted because I was just getting use to not communicating with her. Didn't she get it? I was on a collision course with death and I didn't have time for a girl, especially her. I later broke down, gave in to my heart, and wrote her. We developed an irrevocable bond that would last until her death. That's strange because back then, I didn't know what girl I wanted. How did I settle on Zipporah and not another? I was talking to two other girls when I entered Viet Nam. At that time I was lost to who I wanted. All three were attractive and my "type." But somehow, through my tour in Viet Nam, that dilemma worked itself out. Minerva wrote regularly but I never felt like answering her letters. (But out of the three girls, I didn't write any girl except Zipporah, and that I did reluctantly because death was on my mind and not life.)

I found myself in the jungles of Viet Nam on patrol, looking to engage the enemy. Prior to the point of contact, a sniper's bullet burst passed my head like a roaring lion. It was so close I thought death was calling my name. We were pinned down in a trench and bullets were zinging and pinging all over the place. A friend of mines got hit and I figured the next bullet had my number on it. But it didn't and so I became a little frustrated. If I was going to die, what was taking so long? I thought maybe they needed a better target. My friends were dying. Why was I still here? I stood up with my machine gun in hand letting the bullets rip. All of a sudden, this voice said (I think it was my voice) "What are you doing, trying to get yourself killed?" At that moment, I spotted a body bag carrying a Marine's body who had been in country less than a month, and in his first firefight, he clocked out. And he didn't survive the return trip. I remembered his last conversation back at camp. We were filling sand bags to refortify our home base position. And he said "I came over here to fight and not fill sand bags." That young Marine got his wish. But I couldn't help but think he could have been and should have been me.

Some days later, being one of the senior Marines in the field, I was selected to lead a patrol to find out where the enemy was. It's about 5am or 6am in the morning and while hiding behind some shrubs, I spotted several Viet Cong, and then more. I'm trying to think what I should do. The thought came to mind to rush them, open fire, and call for backup. But I didn't. My thoughts and body froze for a moment or two. I thought about my life, Zipporah, Minerva, Judy and the families of the Marines with me. If Zipporah hadn't written me, when she did, no telling how our lives would have ended that day. I probably would have open fire then called for backup and ended a lot of marines lives

The Master's Call

What do you call this "Fate"? I don't know; and surely, at that age, I had no idea.

While in the field, I received a bit of bad news. "Colgate",, as we called him because of his bright white teeth, caught the train called death. I was depressed and despondent beyond words. This man was my friend and now he was gone. After that news, I really didn't feel much like living. Another patrol called my name. It was about mid-day of the first day out, and about 114 degrees in the shade. Earlier that day, a marine had lost his leg in a booby trap. We were on high alert as we climbed that hill. Near the top, I turned aside to take care of some personal business. I felt something tug at my ankle; I looked down and there was a wire connected to a live grenade, one more step and I would have been history. Why did I detect that small wire that day? Many others had touched such wires and were shipped home in body bags. After such an experience, you walk and sleep light because death could literally be a step and breathe away. Why had I cheated death and lived to talk about it? I didn't know but I was more convinced than ever that I wouldn't get out of Viet Nam alive. I guess you could say, when I received the news that two other close friends bit the bullet, I was screaming mad. But what could I do about it? Nothing, perhaps live a life of bitter regret. Something was keeping me alive but I didn't have time to think about what.

Back at the unit, home base, I finally began celebrate because I was getting short (I had less than thirty days in country); my tour of duty was coming to an end. In all the excitement, I was holding a hand grenade launcher. I pulled the trigger and a grenade sails across a rice paddy and landed a couple feet from an occupied family home. Boy was I in fear. I came feet from injuring or killing the occupants. And since the occupants were friendly, a court-martial could have been my destiny. But in a few days I caught the first thing "smoking" headed for the USA. As I flew across the ocean, I thought how did I get out alive? I had cheated death and lived to talk about it. What do I do now?

Chapter 4

THE MASTER'S CALL

I was discharged from the military, settled in the Washington DC area and tested out for my GED. I married Zipporah and worked as a correctional officer. I took the test for the police force and passed, but I was tired of guns, shooting and killing. The job as a correctional officer paid well but I grew tired physically struggling with inmates and being cursed daily by inmates. I thought there had to be more to life than this. I was very happy with Zipporah but there had to be more to life than this. The position of a senior correctional officer paid well, but I thought it was a dehumanizing job. Zipporah, by this time, was pregnant with our first of two. We had a girl full fun and life. I began to wonder what purpose, other than Zipporah and our baby Nikia did my life hold.

One day I recall when Zipporah and I were walking through the Mall. We heard some spiritual singing. We walked closer to investigate. A church group was singing and offering free Bible classes. They had a booth set up with an electronic score board so you could see how well you scored. I tested my knowledge; I was surprised. I almost scored a hundred percent. With that score, I was ready for the big league. I gave them my name and address and invited them into my home for a Bible study.

One day after that encounter at the Mall, I was driving and passed this moderate looking church building. It was within walking distance from where I lived. But something about that building drew my attention. Every time I passed that building, I became more curious. Who were these people and what did they believe. Although I knew nothing of this church, I found myself praying, "Lord, if you want me to attend this church, wake me up Sunday morning in time for me to attend." (I worked the evening shift and there was no way I was going to wake up at 9 a.m. to attend worship. I had not awakened that early before.)

The Master's Call

Sure enough that Sunday, I woke up a little before 10 a.m. Feeling boxed in, I dressed and went to worship. I felt a little strange there, nothing was as I hoped. The singing, the preaching and the people were different. They sung beautifully, but there was no piano or drums. The preacher came forth to preach, but he didn't have on a preacher's robe. I thought at first he was one of the men coming forth to make an announcement. And when he spoke, I was surprised. I could actually understand every word of his sermon. There was a projector with an overhead format. This visual affect really helped me understand the lesson. This was in the mid-seventies when the relationship between Blacks and Whites was strained. And did I mention the preacher was White and there were quite a few Blacks who attended that church. (This was something else that pointed out how different these people were. There were some older Whites who behaved as if they enjoyed being around Blacks. It wasn't an inconvenience, it was natural). I told myself I would be back.

The next day was Monday, my off day. A White couple came from the church to visit—not to study. I surely enjoyed their company and hoped they enjoyed mines. Isn't it funny how things and people just show up in your life? One minute you are driving to a familiar place, and the next moment, you are visiting some unfamiliar people who slowly begin to change your life. I attended several more times and signed up for a Bible study. Later I discovered this was the same group that sung in the Mall. How weird and unnatural was this?

They sent a beautiful Black couple, Tom and Carol Riley, to study with us. I was somewhat disappointed. Why didn't they send that White couple I met earlier? But what did it matter? It made no difference to God; so it shouldn't make a difference to me. Over the next three months, I studied with Tom and Carol and visited other churches in the area. But something kept pulling me back to that church and those people. I was getting a little agitated. Their questions were beginning to making me feel uncomfortable and guarded. So, I fired back with questions of my own. (Who did they think they were messing with anyway, a Bible knucklehead? I would show them how stupid I was on their next visit). My questions didn't seem to shake them. So I thought it was time to divide and conquer. I knew what the political climate was between most men and women. The man sought to lead, but most women weren't having anything to do with that cave man mentality. I said shrewdly to Carol, "Do you mind being in subjection to your husband?" (I got her now. I thought.) She sprang back, "Not at all." It's amazing how you never forget some people and their answers. I knew then I would never forget this couple.

Shortly thereafter, I submitted to the gospel and my wife followed a week or two later. From that point forward, I was like a sponge soaking up everything in eye and ear range. I called the preacher, Floyd Williamson daily with Bible questions. I couldn't get enough of the Word. I was starving for the Word. But that picture of my grandfather was running through my head. I didn't want to become part of religious hypocrites. I told myself I loved what I was learning, but how does one live this kind of life? Then the answer came from a text I had read, "for by grace are ye saved through faith; and that not of yourselves: it is the gift of God" (Ephesians 2:8 KJV). The idea was we don't and can't live it on our own; it is the blood and Spirit of Christ that helps us live that life pleasing to God.

Chapter 5

LIFE ISN'T MAKING SENSE

I thought a lot about my life, but little was making sense. I was a Christian but not the Christian my grandfather raised me up to be. I wasn't in the same church as was my grandfather. What's going on here? I was confused. How do you figure out what's happening in your life when you have no earthly idea where you are or where you are going? After my conversion I continued asking the preacher questions about the Bible. He finally referred me to one of the Deacons in the church who became my special advisor and tutor. He just happened to be a graduate of the Sunset School of Preaching, a small Bible College in West Texas.

I wouldn't know until later what a major part this deacon and the Sunset would play in my life.

One day out of the blue, the deacon asked if I had given any thought to attending a school of preaching; I told him, no. (I wanted to become a student of the Scriptures and not a preacher.) During that time, I had given a lot of thought to my career as a Correctional Officer. I knew I didn't want to do that long term. The job was too violent, unsafe and too depriving of human qualities. I was a Correctional Officer and I was in charge of a cell block. On a particular day, my cell block was scheduled to see a movie in the mess hall. I generally attended the movie with the inmates from my unit. However, that day, I was trying to do the Christian thing of watching what my eyes beheld. I appoint another officer to go. About half way through the movie, I heard a loud noise of unrest. I looked out the barred windows and saw an inmate wearing an officer's hat and coat. My first thought was a riot had taken place; the inmates were now in charge. And as I suspected, inmates had taken over the mess hall and were holding officers hostage. Within minutes, the Command Center initiated an emergency plan to contain and end the riot. But by the time control had been reestablished and the officers freed, several of the officers suffered an acute psychiatric disorder. After that experience, they were unable to continue to work in the system. As I thought about the officer from my unit, my thoughts were that officer could have been me. Those officers were never the same; nor was I. I made up my mind that day: I didn't care how much the job paid. The job had to go. I often wondered why I didn't give in and go to the movie that day. I wanted to but I didn't. I later learned the movie was decent for a change. What if I was that officer? Would I have survived the take over? I shuddered to think.

In the mean time, the deacon who was seeking to persuade me to attend a school of preaching succeeded. The daily stress of my job was working against me. I thought maybe God would give me a better job if I chose to enter this Bible College. I made up my mind I would, but not before I talked it over with Zipporah. She surprised me—she agreed. I told the elders of the church of our decision. They were elated but a little skeptical with a few reservations. Before departing, they gave us some of the best parenting advice we had received to date. "Before punishing your daughter, make sure you both agree." Why? Not properly communicating with your spouse could hurt and even destroy your marriage; plus to do otherwise would not have been an example of biblical love. Zipporah and I followed that advice in raising both of our children (Nikia and Ian). Praise the Lord. They turned out pretty good.

Chapter 6

HEADED INTO THE UNKNOWN

We packed up and headed towards Lubbock Texas. We called ahead to let the school know we were coming, but in haste we fail to make reservations where we would stay. We were so happy to be going to college we forgot to make living arrangements. We arrived in Lubbock late that evening and the school was closed. So, I called one of the instructors, a number I just happened to have. The instructor asked where were we? And it just so happen, we were no more than a few blocks from his house. He invited us to stay the night and we would house hunt in the morning. The next day we didn't go house hunting. Richard and his wife invited us to stay in their home as long as we liked. The wife and I felt so blessed. We ask ourselves "Who does this without hesitation?" The answer was obvious and touching. Our lives had been touch and blessed by New Testament Christians. We accepted their gracious invitation, and when we finally got a place of our own, Richard said some of the most profound words I ever heard. He looked at me and said "You have one of the sharpest minds I ever met. God has great things in store for you and Zipporah." I wondered who he was talking about. Not me, because the Steve I knew had a dull mind, and there was nothing great about him. I had problems keeping up with my normal course load. But I never forgot Richard, his family or his generous words.

I graduated from Sunset and went on to graduate school. I was chosen to be the commencement speaker for my class. And I might add, I was the only Black student in the class. As part of the exit strategy, all students were required to appear before the elders and discuss what their exit plans were. When it came my turn, I was extremely nervous; I had no idea what I would do. And I told the review board the same. After graduate school, maybe I would return to

Washington, DC get a job and work when I could in the church but no preaching Job. I wasn't ready and after I learned the responsibilities of a preacher. I thought I would never be ready. One of the elders on the committee suggested I try preaching. I almost fainted. I told him I didn't want to be a preacher and felt I wasn't preaching material. There was nothing in me that would make a good preacher (I felt a little like my grandfather. I needed to get my life together.

I went on to graduate school after completing that program. I stood ready for a new task. Once again I was faced with preaching and again I said no. Then something inside of me said, (it probably was me talking to me), "why don't you try preaching?" Reluctantly, I decided to give preaching a try. But nothing in me said I would like preaching or do well as a preacher. So I entered preaching with the attitude of failure. And at my first congregation, I fail miserably. I seriously thought about quitting, and did for a few days, until I received an unexpected call from a congregation asking me to come and work with them. I conferred with a friend, Lloyd Harris. He helped me to make an otherwise difficult choice as to whether or not I would remain in the ministry. But my real plan was to work with this a congregation for a few years and then get a job outside the ministry. I don't know why but preaching and I were like oil and water.

But it seem like something wouldn't let me alone. I wanted to get out but I couldn't see my way out. It was like something wouldn't let me out and blocked my every move to slip out. I felt a little like Jeremiah in 20:9 (KJV). "Then I said, I will not make mention of him, nor speak any more in his name. But his word was in mine heart as a burning fire shut up in my bones, and I was weary with forbearing, and I could not stay." I kept on preaching but preaching wasn't in me. Something kept pushing me forward. I really didn't have it in me. But I remembered the open door God opened when I resigned from my first work. It wasn't a week before that call came requesting me to consider working with another congregation. I didn't inquire or seek it; the door just open. I accepted that second work with serious reservations.

After ten years, I resigned from that work. I didn't feel I was doing this church or me any real spiritual good. However, that wasn't the census of the congregation. When some learned I was thinking of leaving, they begged me to stay. But I told myself this church can get along without and could do better than me; so I quit. So I quit. I was working as a therapist in a prison hospital, and the salary was generous. I finally quit the ministry and I was happy. But another call came from a congregation I knew nothing about. Robert James, a dear friend of mine's, learned this church was looking for a minister, and he gave them my name and phone number. And since Robert had given this church my contact information, I decided to contact them so they could look elsewhere. I decided to visit with them but still having no intentions of working with them. I did and it seemed to me that this church would be a good work for someone. But again, I really wasn't interested. I returned home and forgot about my visit and my impression of them. But the leadership hadn't forgotten me. They called me back for another visit. They offered me the job. I told them I would need to think about it. I thought and prayed about it. I asked myself, was God pushing me toward this ministry? But I wasn't interested. Robert and I talked about the work, and he gave me his reasons why I should seriously consider the work. I thought about it, prayed about it and looked for a way out of it. Robert reassured me, urging me to accept the work. Robert was an older preacher and had far more experience with God and the ministry. So I decided to take his advice. Robert James is gone to be with the Lord. And after sixteen years, I have never regretted that decision to work with this congregation. Is there another name for what's happening in my life? Maybe it's providence?

Chapter 7

THE CANCER RETURNED

My wife was diagnosed with ovarian cancer. She completed her treatments but she didn't get any better. We first discovered she had cancer more than twenty years ago. We thought she had beaten it but I guess not. I asked God to extend her life and he did. He gave her another ten years. Later, she would die. I was angry, bitter and afraid. I thought I would never marry again. But later the Lord would put a sister, Evelyn Kaye in my life; I couldn't say no. I eventually married Kaye and the first few years were difficult but worth it. Kaye helped me get over my loss. Our lives have bonded well with time, experience and love. The Lord gave us both another chance at love. I am glad we took that chance because we are better for it. The Lord gave me a miracle in marrying Zipporah; then gave me another miracle in marrying Kaye. Who says "Miracles have ceased?"

I recall once, when traveling to a Doctor's appointment out of town, I fell asleep, wandered off the road driving over sixty mph. The car was almost totaled, but I walked away without a scratch. That crash taught me a very important lesson, never count God out or take him for granted. He delivers us while we are sleeping in life.

Allow me to regress for a moment to show you how good God is. I applied for a job with the state prison in Parham Mississippi. I was still preaching and ran an outside clinic on weekends once or twice a month in Milan Illinois. I was at the clinic on an extended weekend and I received a call from the personnel office in Mississippi asking me to come in for an interview. I was twelve plus hours from Mississippi and didn't see the need of cutting my trip short. But there was a pressure in my spirit to go so I did. When I got there for the interview, there were between two to five openings and twenty-five or more applicants.

At first my thought was with these few positions I should have stayed in Milan. I was in Mississippi and my paranoia about Mississippi kicked in.

This was Mississippi, and Mississippi had a "Good Old Boy system." "If you are Black, step back and don't look back." They called me in for my interview, and it was as I suspected, all White and one woman on the board. I probably thought to myself, boy, are you wasting your time! But to my astonishment, I was hired. The woman on the board casted the deciding vote. The position was for a case manager. How did I make the cut? Maybe they thought they were going to get a therapist for a case manager salary. And that was a fifteen thousand dollar difference. Over the next five years, I worked as a case manager in a Special Needs Unit. All inmates assigned to me received medication and therapy from the hospital staff. Consequently, I got to know very well. One therapist learned I worked as a counselor on the outside. He vowed he would get me into the hospital as a therapist. I said sure. But there was a problem; the hospital administrator didn't like me. I don't know why. Could it have been the color of my skin? All I know is the woman who had cast her vote in my favor; she was his wife and she had no ill-will toward me (There was nothing romantic between us, she just believed in giving Blacks a level playing field). And sure enough, an opening came for a Psych Therapist. I applied and was called in for an interview. I passed and was hired. The therapist, who said he would help me get the position didn't get me hired but he helped because there were two or more others on the board he couldn't sway. They appeared to be men who made their own judgment. But someone had placed me on their minds. After all there were more qualified applicants than myself.

I thought all my troubles were over until I learned that the Hospital Administrator didn't want to start me at the regular pay grade of a therapist. He wanted me to start at a lower pay grade than others. I learned about this through the grapevine (Everyone talks in prison you just have to find the right vine). I told that person I expected to make the same beginning salary as other therapists. My source said I will see if I can make it happen. I don't know how, but it happened. That invisible force was still at work. You would think as a preacher, I would have connected the dots as to what was happening to me, but I didn't. I guess I was too busy condemning myself for past failures. I guess this is why the story of David always fascinated me. After all David had done all those things that displeased the Lord, including murder. But God still called him a man after his heart. We will never be perfect on our own, but God knows when we are trying and when we are taking him for granted. Jesus counts us as righteous by the shedding of his blood and the extension of his grace. This is why things work out, when they shouldn't, and this is why we receive blessings when we should receive cursing. This is why God calls sinners into the ministry. We don't deserve it but grace covers what we lack.

Chapter 8

NOTHING COMES EASY

Nothing about preaching came easy or natural for me. But counseling came effortless and non-problematic. It was like putting on a tailored suit. I guess you could say counseling came with a natural fit.

It is like one tranquil morning a middle-age woman burst into my office. I was in shock, wondering what did I do to deserve this. She appeared to be going through a psychotic episode. I noticed she appeared agitated and unable to hold a normal conversation without crying and looking overwhelmed. Later I learned she was undergoing a panic attack. I calmly talked with her until I was able to establish the identity of her doctor. I called him, with her permission, and informed him what was happening. He agreed to see her and he would refill her medication. On another occasion, a person called talking of suicide. I knew I was supposed to call and alert the "authorities" but he kept me on the line and refused to hang up. I asked him why he wanted to commit suicide. He gave me several answers but none made any real sense. I decided I wouldn't characterize or identify any of his answers as unreasonable or vacuous. I thought this would only agitate him more. Instead, I told him I understood his point and asked if he would consider a few things he hadn't considered. He asked "what?" So I gave him some alternatives to death and reasons why he should at least consider them. When he appeared calm, I referred him to medical help with an escort.

I would be the first to say that all problems are not so easily resolved, and when in doubt, always seek the help of a professional. When it came to counseling, things often fell into place. Now it appeared I was beginning to see that there was something unusual at work in me. But I kept it to myself. I often told myself not to get in over my head. I knew I was dealing with people and their lives; the last thing I wanted to do was shipwreck someone's life.

I have learned that a great deal of counseling was related to a good deal of common sense (this is not to say training isn't warranted). If you have common sense, you are going to be able to help a lot of people out there. And if you don't, a lot of people are going to suffer. Was I predetermined, destined to become a counselor? For as much as I know, there was something happening in my life, but I didn't understand what. However, just because I didn't understand what was happening, didn't mean God wasn't at work in my life. You would think after thirty years of ministering and counseling I would know someone was at work in me beyond my self. Someone said "Believing it's going to rain and knowing it, are two different things." One could say it was raining in my life but I didn't recognize it. I guess I was more observant of what or who was working in others' lives than my own.

Chapter 9

AM I CONVINCED?

What about being called to preach? I am afraid the verdict isn't in on that. Personally, I am still a little twisted in both counseling and preaching. But if I wasn't destined to preach, I have spent thirty-five years of my life doing something God never call me to do. Isn't that scary? But isn't there another name for it? What about destined, purposed, predetermined, ordained or called? One of the purposes of this book is for the reader to look back on his or her life and see the hand of God at work in areas one never noticed. And when you see those occasions, you will probably see more reasons to praise him than doubt him. You will see more prayers answered than those you thought were ignored and unanswered.

I think it would be very helpful if you seriously considered your own ministry. First and foremost, if Jesus Christ is Saviour and Lord in your life, the rest doesn't matter; but if he's not, things that ought not to matter in life will matter and consume you. Accept a little brotherly advice here; turn your life over to Jesus. You can trust him as promised in Romans "We know that all things work together for good of those who love God: those who are called according to his purpose" (Romans 8:28 HCSB). The message of Romans is God assures us of deliverance (freedom) from suffering—through Christ. This is the whole point of all that has been written thus far.

> Man desperately struggles against the pressures and forces from both within and without. He struggles against the weight and discouragement of trials against the pollution and the corruption of life against the relentless accusations and bombardments of conscience and law against the pain and decay of his body and against the striking fear and hopelessness of eternal judgment in

hereafter. He struggles against the unknown and against pain, hurt, sorrow, loneliness, alienation, aging, death, and hell (Jenkins, "Peace in the Midst of Peril"). (Compare this with Galatians 5:17-18 KJV).

Somehow through man's suffering and struggles throughout life, he feels that his suffering and struggles maybe *due to a wrong relationship with God.*

Therefore, man views his many problems as *really* being one supreme problem: how do I get right with God? If only man could establish the right relationship with God, they would feel surer of God's help, protection and provisions in life.

This is the very message of Romans. Man needs to get right with God, for he is under the condemnation and the wrath of God (Romans 1:18,3:20 KJV). Man needs to be in a right relationship with God; he needs to be justified; that is, declared righteous by God (Romans 3:21,5:21 KJV). Man needs to be freed from the struggle of sin, for sin corrupts and leads to death (Romans 6:1-23 KJV). Man needs to be freed from the bondage of law (spiritual legalism) for the law enslaves, accuses, condemns, and strikes hopelessness within the heart of man (Romans 7:1-25 KJV). But know this; God will work out whatever has our backs against the wall, and work it out for good and God's glory (Preacher's Outline and Sermon Bible).

Chapter 10

A THERAPIST OR PREACHER?

People have problems, pure and simple. But whom should we go to in order to get help resolving our crises, a professional therapist or a preacher? Should a Christian with personal and mental problems seek help from a Professional Mental Health provider or a pastor? This became confusing and an obstacle to me as a young minister. Who do you turn to when the problem is clearly outside your training, scope and ability? Christian ministers face this struggle every day in their ministry. One of the reasons I enrolled in graduate school was to seek help in resolving this question in my ministry.

For example, imagine one day a young Christian man in his late twenties comes to you and admits he's schizophrenic and gay and requests guidance. Do you seek to counsel him or refer him?

While each case is different, and there are no easy answers, here are a few guidelines I believe will be helpful. One day, a young man I had known for some time came into my office and dropped "trouble" in my lap. He confessed a secret he had carried for a number of years. He stated he was gay. I had known this young man for more than seven years. I was speechless. I thought surely I would have known if he was gay, but I hadn't. Usually ministers and pastors have a firm knowledge of the Bible and how it applies to people's lives. But I had no idea where to start this conversation. This brother was asking me to counsel him on this subject and to keep our sessions private. I prayed about it and decided to discuss the love of God before discussing his condition. Afterwards he left satisfied and glad he had sought counseling on this matter.

Such experiences should teach us not to get in over our heads in matters we do not fully understand and are not fully equipped to serve. It's easy to hurt those we are trying to help because we don't have a commanding knowledge of the problem or condition at hand. I like Paul's approach to resolving conflict. He sought to "become all things to all men" that he might win, secure or save some (1 Cor. 9:22 NKJV). However, though we seek to become all things to all men, we differ in individual talents and abilities (Matt 25:15 KJV). God does not expect us to use talents we do not possess. Would we hire a carpenter to fix a plumbing problem or seek treatment from a Dentist for a broken arm? All I am saying is skill, ability and the severity of the problem should dictate where we go for help. There was a time, when I was trying to be a Jack of all trades but a master of none. This was both confusing to me and hurtful to any potential client. It wasn't long before I began to feel "burnt out" and my ministry suffered, especially in the area of sermon preparation (In the pulpit I began to think and speak more like a therapist than a preacher of the gospel). I was seeking to provide counseling in areas I should have provided the Word. It was only after I returned to graduate school did I discover how potentially dangerous I had become. A little knowledge is a dangerous thing. All problems usually have a spiritual and physical component and when we lack that insight, we can do more harm than good. We seek to place a band-aid over a major wound.

When it comes to Christians specifically, who should they bring their problems to, a clinical professional or their pastor? Often there is a need for both. The pastor takes care of those problems relating to sin and one's relationship with God. After all, did not Jesus say "But when Jesus heard that, he said unto them, they that be whole need not a physician, but they that are sick" (Matt. 9:12 KJV). Jesus warned, as a physician, he had come to aid the spiritually sick. He had come to earth for the same purpose that a physician enters a home: to help the sick. However, just like the physician, He came to minister to the sick who called him into their homes for healing. Jesus is also warning the self-righteous he came to have mercy and not to lead people to make sacrifices. What Jesus wants is not our sacrifices, but the wholeness of our lives in his service. He came to show and bestow mercy upon sinners. Jesus warned that He came to call sinners to repentance. If a person does not know he needs changing (repenting), he cannot be helped. We cannot receive help in areas of acute mental illness by calling a preacher with no experience or training outside the Scriptures. We must acknowledge the problem exists and the specific skills we need to help resolve them.

An Oncologist is preferred over a general practitioner when treating cancer; a licensed therapist is usually preferred over a minister when dealing with matters of mental health because these are usually beyond the minister's training and ability. A minister is primarily a Gospel preacher and Bible teacher—not a counselor specializing in all areas of mental health. Why do we seek medical advice from those qualified in medicine when dealing with medical issues, and not preachers? Ministers usually concentrate and seek to aid relatively healthy people who are encountering situational crises in their personal lives. However, spiritual counseling is not always enough. Sometimes, it requires a licensed therapist. If this is the case, it is important that ministering counselors have a data base of reliable and trained therapists who (they trust) who can help with specific problems beyond the minister's experience and training. The error among some pastors is they fail to recognize the need for such therapists in their ministry. "Let us not therefore judge one another anymore: but judge this rather, that no man put a stumbling block or an occasion to fall in his brother's way" (Rom 13:14 KJV). Brothers and sisters can be denied appropriate care because we judge them rather than seek to aid them.

In my ministry I have learned some people do better in the hands of the professional. I learned some people need medicine before they can be approached with talk therapy. Some people are delusional and without medication could be a danger to themselves as well as the pastor.

Chapter 11

KNOW YOUR LIMITATIONS

Remember all counseling has its limitations, so make sure you know your limitations for the benefit of the person needing help, as well as yourself. We should all know our limitations.

> And the evil spirit answered and said, Jesus I know, and Paul I know; but who are ye? And the man in whom the evil spirit was leaped on them, and overcame them, and prevailed against them, so that they fled

out of that house naked and wounded (Acts 19:15-16 KJV).

It is the role of the spiritual counselor to facilitate change in the spiritual area of a client's life. The greatest gift a pastoral counselor can give to a client is a listening ear, an open heart and a relative word from the Lord. Is there another word or name that describes why ministers and pastoral counselors do what they do? I think some who believe in themselves and having been "called" think they can do no wrong. Peter was "called" but he was still wrong.. "But when Peter was come to Antioch, I withstood him to the face, because he was to be blamed" (Galatians 2:11 KJV). I refer a lot more people than I use to because I do not wish to be blamed.

I received a call from a minister friend asking me if I would talk to one of his family members. After talking with that person somewhat in-depth, I suspected medication might helpful and the MMP-I (Minnesota Multiphasic Personality Inventory) should be considered to confirm a pre diagnosis. I have had some training in administering and reading the MMPI. So I administered the test, read it and referred him to mental health with my personal notes. I continued to help him with his spiritual concerns. He is back working and doing much better. Praise God. The team approach worked for this person. However, I try not to refer people to those I don't know. Most, in my opinion, do not need or warrant referrals. Counseling to me is all about helping people. But if we can't help, we shouldn't hinder them from receiving proper help.

Few of us would try to practice medicine without a license; it is equally important that we as pastoral counselors do not practice psychotherapy without certification or a license. We should help those who need help in the area of our knowledge, training and confidence. (Some material used here was written by Brumet, "Spiritual and Psychological Counseling.")

Chapter 12

AN INTEREST OR DESTINY?

How do you determine if you have an interest or a destiny? If you have an interest, it probably appeals to you and a few others and is local in scope. If it's a destiny, it appeals to you, it helps others, and the scope has no boundaries. Interest is in our area of control, but destiny is usually out of our control, except in personal choice. If it's an interest, we mean to do it; if it's a destiny, we make a choice to do it. Interest usually deals with our present; but destiny deals with our past, present and future. Interest says it matters only what happens to us; but destiny says it only matters how we react to what happens to us. Interest says we choose how we live; destiny says we have some choices in how we live.

Obviously, I disagree with part of this premise. I don't believe you can completely separate interest, choice and destiny. In order to have destiny, you must have the freedom to explore your interest in making choices. Listen to Jeremiah the prophet conversation with God:

> Before I formed thee in the belly I knew thee; and before thou camest forth out of the womb I sanctified thee, and I ordained thee a prophet unto the nations. Then said I, Ah, Lord GOD! Behold, I cannot speak: for I am a child. But the LORD said unto me, Say not, I am a child: for thou shalt go to all that I shall send thee, and whatsoever I command thee thou shalt speak (Jeremiah 1:5-7 KJV).

God told Jeremiah that He ordained, predetermined him to be a prophet. Did Jeremiah have a choice? Yes. He chose to stop preaching for a season (Jeremiah 20:9 KJV). Another thing God told Jeremiah was not only did he call him; he also equipped him for the job (Jeremiah 1:6-7 KJV). Since equipping is the same as calling, those who are equipped are also called.

If you believe in destiny, you believe there is a greater force at work in defining your life. There is choice in destiny. My life is not one I observe from a distance, but one I participate in up close; I am making daily choices that affect my destiny and lead me to my destiny. "Sometimes we make choices in life and sometimes choices make us" (Forman, p. 161). Yes God has a destiny for my life and I have choices in my destiny. Joshua says, "And if it seem evil unto you to serve the LORD, choose you this day whom ye will serve" (Joshua 24:15 KJV). We daily have personal choices to serve evil or do good. And whatever my destiny might be its interwoven with my choices. For example, God desires that all men be saved and come to the knowledge of the truth. But despite God's will, God will never force us to be saved against our individual will. This is what the Apostle Paul wrote of in Ephesians "For we are his workmanship, created in Christ Jesus unto good works, which God hath before ordained [predetermined] that we should walk in them" (Ephesians 2:10 KJV). What did God ordain or predetermine? All who would be saved would be saved "in Christ." We are God's workmanship, created in Christ Jesus. The Christian experiences two creations, both a natural and a spiritual birth. The spiritual birth is the point of this verse. When a man obeys Jesus Christ, God *creates him in Christ*. What does this means? It means that God *quicken the spirit* of the Christian and makes his spirit alive in us. Whereas man's spirit was dead to God but now it's alive through Jesus. What does this have to do with choice and destiny? We choose to be transformed and God continues to work his plan in our lives but always by our choice..

> "And we know that all things *work together for good* to them that love God, to them who are the called according to *his* purpose[22] (Romans 8:28 KJV).

The words "work together" are present action, which means that all things *are continually* working together for good. God is in control of the Christian's life. Daily, moment by moment, God is arranging and rearranging all things for the Christian's good. The word "good" (*agathon*) means for the *ultimate* good. We cannot see the future; we cannot take a single event and see all the lines and ramifications that run from it. We cannot see all the things that result from one single event, much less see the results of every event. But God does; therefore, God takes all the events of our lives and works them out for our *ultimate* good (*Romans*, Preacher's Outline and Sermon Bible). How is that for choice and destiny? I chose to enter the military (but I didn't choose Viet Nam, PTSD or Agent Orange). I chose to marry (but I didn't choose for my wife to become ill and die). I chose to seek God. I chose to enter graduate school, but I didn't choose some of the things that came along with those choices.

For example, I learned of a young sister who was involved in an accident. I inquired and learned she was well but the vehicle she drove was totaled and aided in saving her life. Suppose she had chosen to drive a smaller car then what? She may not still be with us. The driver of the other vehicle, on the other hand, was seriously injured and sustained life-threatening injuries. I visited with him once out of I.C.U. He revisited the scene of the accident in his mind. He told me that he had complained to the doctor that something wasn't right with him but he was told everything was going to be fine. He made a choice to get in his car and drive. He says he blanked out. He doesn't remember the accident except waking up in the ER being told by a medical staff member he needed emergency surgery. He says the only thing he remembered about the accident was someone or something placing their arms around him. And that person or thing saved his life. He praised God for the next twenty minutes non-stop. He says he is still alive because God must have something for him to do. His choice pointed out that he has a destiny. And he would have never known it if he had not had that life-threatening accident. His choice connected him to his destiny, and I suppose my choices did the same. We can make a wrong choice and still, sometimes, get to the right place in spite of our choice. But this is only true if it be the determined will and foreknowledge of God. Usually, wrong choices lead to wrong decisions, and wrong decisions lead to wrong paths and wrong paths can lead to a misunderstand of God's will for our lives.

Thinking back on Minerva and Zipporah, I had to make a choice. If I had married Minerva, I am persuaded my life would have been different. Our children would have been different, where we lived would have been different and our faith and where we worshipped God would have been different. Family has always played an important part in the decision making. And, if my family was uncomfortable with a decision, I would revisit that decision just to make sure I hadn't missed anything that would possibly lead me to make a different. I am not saying all my decisions were right, but I did all I could to make them right. I evaluate and reevaluated the information before me to make a reasonable informed decision. The point is family and environment impact our decisions about God. A different family could very well change where our relationship is with God. Nevertheless, the choices I made set me on this course where I would collide with God. I am convinced I am on the right path. But will I make the right choices on this path? Am I making the right choices and is God influencing my choices as I make them? God said concerning Pharaoh "And in very deed for this cause have I raised thee up, for to shew in thee my power; and that my name may be declared throughout all the earth" (Exodus 9:16 KJV). It is clear God had a hand in Pharaoh's life. Yes Pharaoh made his own choices but God used those choices to glorify Himself. Does God use our choices to bring glorify to himself? Yes. I made my own choices that brought about specifics changes in my life and in the lives of others. God was free to use those choices in ways I never intended to please himself because I belong to him.

Destiny is the outcome of all the choices we make. Our choices only pave the path that was already here.

> But here's the painful part: You can miss God's destiny for your life. People do it all the time. In fact, you can go through your entire life and miss God's purpose for your life—by your own choices. If you choose to chase pleasure, popularity, or money instead of God, you'll miss it [God's destiny for your life]. And that's tragic.
>
> God's will is not automatic. He allows us to make choices. Many of the things that happen to you are not God's perfect will. We all have to choose between God's will and our will....

But you can have God's will for your life. Even when you mess up, God can turn disaster into destiny (Warren, "Your Destiny, Your Choice").

God gives us a destiny despite our cursing Him, despite our rejecting Him, despite our rebelling against Him, despite our hostility toward Him, despite our denial of Him, despite our neglect of Him, despite our half-hearted commitment to Him, despite our false worship, and despite our trespasses and sins. Destiny is a matter of choice. It is not a thing to wait for, it is a thing to be achieved (Bryan, *Brainy Quotes*).

I remember the slaying of nine Blacks in a church in South Carolina. The murderer intended to kill those he killed, but he didn't intend for the confederate flag to fall. In the same way, God uses our decisions to achieve his will. And if this is so, there must be another name for it. When my daughter was between three and four years old, she came into my study and I picked her up and asked, "Are you going to marry a preacher?" She looked at me and burst my bubble saying "No." I guessed I worked too much and stayed away from home too long for my daughter to ever consider marrying a preacher. That day, my daughter made a decision for herself, the husband and the children she would never have. To this day, Nikia has never married nor does she have children. My son, Ian Patrick, is married and has one child. Something I have noticed about him he expresses no desire to preach. I think he would make a good preacher if he ever developed a desire and acquired the necessary skills. I wonder why me and why not him? He looks like me, talks like me, but I guess he is not totally like me. Although I don't think I chose the ministry, as much as the ministry chose me. I am grateful for the decisions my children have made. Though my son hasn't chosen the ministry, and the ministry hasn't chosen him, I am so grateful what my children have given God—their lives. May the Lord bless them to keep them in the precious faith.

Chapter 13

SHE FELL ASLEEP, AND I LEARNED A VALUABLE LESSON

My mother died and I wept. My father died and a dull pain appeared to seize me. Zipporah, my wife died, and I screamed, sinking into a deep sorrow and an ominous pain. There is suppose to be a lesson in the death, but what is the lesson? What is the message that seems to evade, escape our minds and hearts? When she died, my world shattered and I began to sink.

I remember it like it was yesterday. A beautiful sunny day dripped from the Master's brush. I was at ease in my pain, but then she stopped breathing, and the pain ripped me to the core. A medical staff tried to comfort me. I recall stating just above a whisper, "Don't touch me." I was angry at God, but I didn't recognize it. I felt raw and all alone in the world.

It has been some time since that spring day Zipporah died and I still find myself asking, "What was the purpose of it all?" I prayed, I carried her from specialist to specialist, hospital to hospital, and she still died. "Lord, I could have lived without the experience of death." But could I? Could any one of us make it to our destiny without the pain and suffering of death? It took death for us to attain life, Jesus' death (Romans 5:10 KJV says, "For if, when we were enemies, we were reconciled to God by the death of his Son, much more, being reconciled, we shall be saved by his life"). Being a Christian doesn't shelter us from "the death experience." Paul says we die daily that we might live (1 Corinthians 15:31). What is the spiritual and physical lesson that death should teach us?

1. We die individually and collectively because of our sin.

2. We try to escape pain, the very thing that helps bring our healing.
3. Healing is elusive, but trusting God brings healing.

We live in a world dominated by sin; therefore, we can't escape sin. So, if we can't escape sin, we must endure the pain of sin, which is often just for a moment. Second Corinthians 4:17 says, "For our light affliction, which is but for a moment, worketh for us a far more exceeding and eternal weight of glory" (KJV). My personal experiences, though painful, are for the manifestation of God's glory in me. In other words, my pain should bring glory to God through me and should cause God to be praised through me.

You see, if I try to escape pain because of its continuous irritation, God doesn't receive His full glory. My attempting to escape says that God is doing something wrong by allowing me to experience death. But without death in our lives, we can't experience the true meaning of eternal life. Yes, I cry in despair like those who have no hope, but I can always trust God to bring healing and eternal life (1 Corinthians 15:15-20).

The lesson that helps us all in death is not about pain and suffering; it's about hope, comfort, joy, and living. Why be angry with God? We blame Him for letting our parents, our spouse, and our children die. All God is saying through death is that they will live again. As a matter of fact, they haven't ceased to live; they have just moved to a different room in His house. God is a good and merciful God. Fret not, you can and will see them again. So, stop your weeping as those who have no hope. You can and will see them again. People die because death is part of living. Beloved, there is not a person living who will not see or be touched by death. Christ has the keys to that dominion we all seek to go.

So, wake up. God isn't punishing us when death visits and it feels like it's more than we can bear. I have learned to hold His hand in the midst of pain; His grace has proven to be sufficient, adequate, enough to wipe away my tears and comfort me with a comfort that passes my comprehension. Second Corinthians 1:4 KJV says, "Who comforteth [consoles] us in all our tribulation, that we may be able to comfort them which are in any trouble, by the comfort wherewith we ourselves are comforted of God" (KJV).

We all go through the various stages or steps of grief:

1. Shock/denial/unbelief
2. Anger at God and others
3. Blame/bargaining with God
4. Depression: I am so alone. I can't bear living with this lost
5. Acceptance: In the midst of it all, God continues to bring His goodness

Once we arrive at accepting God's will, we release the pain and accept the joy of His will. Our faculties are so much clearer. Our appetites and sleep have returned and so has our joy. In grief, good can come. God moved in our darkness to point us to His light. He taught me that my wife was not my only purpose for living. There were persons, yet alive, who needed my guidance. They are weary in darkness, looking for the light. And He would send another to comfort my heart and uplift my soul. Kaye, my second wife, did that and more. Kaye's love has lifted and reinvigorated me to continue God's work.

SOME FINAL WORDS

Thank you for allowing this old soldier to think out aloud in your presence. I know you have better things to do, but thank you for sharing your time, your ear, and an open heart with me. Before I started this written journey, there was a time I had serious reservations and questions about the ministry and I was truly puzzled. But God has been good and answered my questions and resolved my doubts and now I have peace of mind and spirit. As someone said, you made "the journey worth the distance." As a matter of fact, without God and you, I would have never made the choice to travel the distance.

Most games have what is called an initiator, a game starter, and a coach who helps us to perform our best to win the game. I thank my grandfather whom God used to initiate this journey. I thank my father who helped me to see that if you pursue your father, he will lead you through the darkness into the light. I thank my mom whose affection for my father taught me human love isn't always perfect but it's always worth the drive. I thank Zipporah whose love taught me disease can weaken and kill the body but it can't destroy love. And Kaye, the love of my life who taught me it is never too late to fall in love if you trust God to send the right person. I thank God for helping me to find you. (By the way, we are still indebted to Mercedes.) Most of all, I thank God for teaching me as he taught Jeremiah, "… Say not, I [am] a child: for thou shalt go to all that I shall send thee, and whatsoever I command thee thou shalt speak" (Jeremiah 1:7 KJV).

I believe since the age of nine, I have known one day I would preach but I hid that thought in the back of my mind and refused to entertain it. After all, I was a child.; I didn't know anything and in my thinking I wasn't good enough. Since that time God has taught me "It's not how good you are or what you know. It's how good God is and what he knows." Don't limit God in what he can do in accomplishing his will in your life. And in this, I rejoice.

The Master's Call Falls Upon Me

REFERENCES

Brumet, Robert. "Spiritual and Psychological Counseling." May 2010. *RobertBrumet.com*.

Bryan, William Jennings. *Brainy Quotes*.

Forman, Gayle. *If I Stay*. New York: Dutton Books, 2009.

Jenkins, Frederick L., Sr. "Peace in the Midst of Peril." June 22, 2009. *Preacherman: Thoughts for Living*. http://preacherman499.blog spot.com/2009/06/peace-in-midst-of-peril.html.

Romans. The Preacher's Outline and Sermon Bible. Chattanooga, TN: Leadership Ministries Worldwide, 1996.

Warren, Rick. "Your Destiny, Your Choice." May 21, 2014. *Daily Hope with Rick Warren*. http://rickwarren.org/devotional/english/your-destiny-your-choice.

www.ingramcontent.com/pod-product-compliance
Lightning Source LLC
Chambersburg PA
CBHW050605300426
44112CB00013B/2073